NELSON MANDELA
THE PRESIDENT WHO SPENT 27 YEARS IN PRISON

Biography for Kids
Children's Biography Books

DISSECTED LIVES
auto biographies

Speedy Publishing LLC

40 E. Main St. #1156

Newark, DE 19711

www.speedypublishing.com

Copyright 2017

Nelson Mandela was an Activist and President in South Africa. He was born in Mvezo, South Africa on July 18, 1918. You may have heard about him serving 27 years in a prison protesting apartheid. He passed away in Johannesburg on December 5, 2013.

Nelson Mandela was a leader of civil rights. He fought in opposition to apartheid, a system that designated non-white citizens be segregated from the whites and they were not equals. He served most of his life in prison because of his protests, becoming a representation for his people. He then became their first black president in 1994.

FREEDOM
PEACE

WHERE DID HE GROW UP?

He was born July 18, 1918 in Mvezo, South Africa. Rolihlaha is his birth name. His father served as counselor to the tribal chiefs but died when he was 9. He was then adopted by Chief Jongintaba Dalindyebo, the Thembu regent.

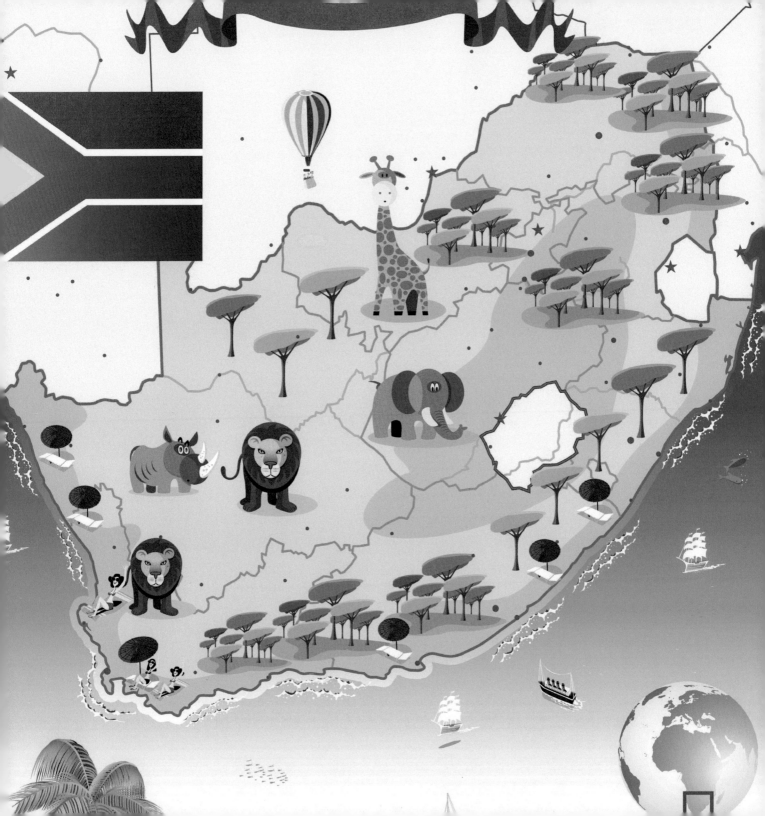

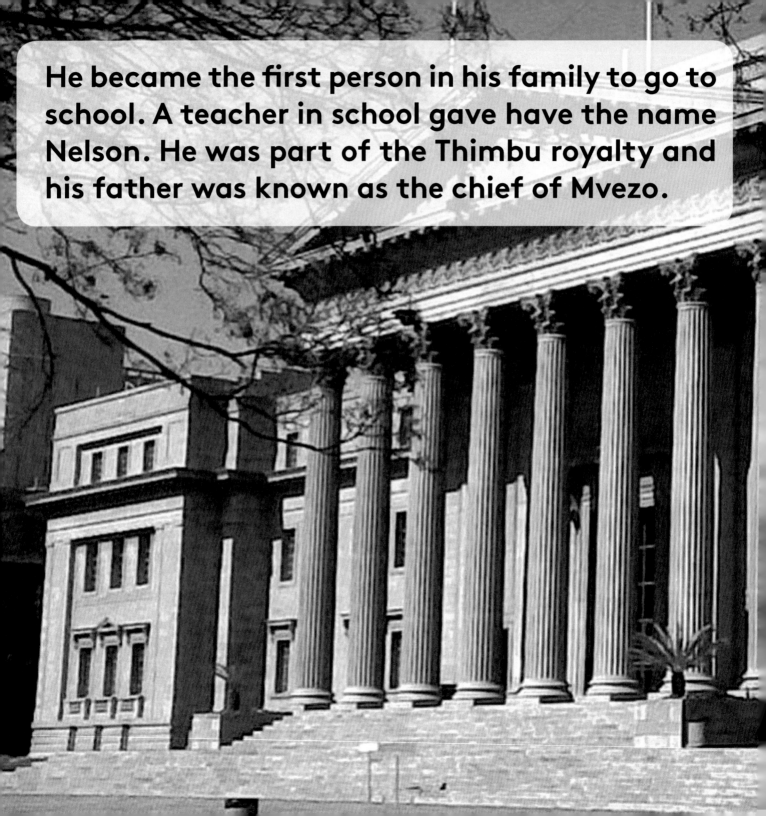

He became the first person in his family to go to school. A teacher in school gave have the name Nelson. He was part of the Thimbu royalty and his father was known as the chief of Mvezo.

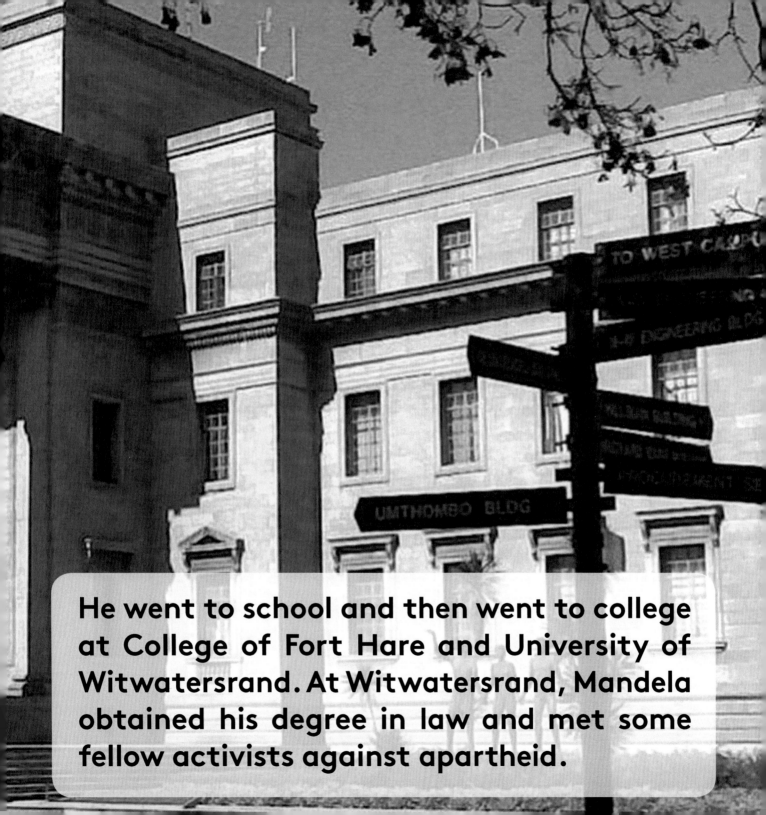

He went to school and then went to college at College of Fort Hare and University of Witwatersrand. At Witwatersrand, Mandela obtained his degree in law and met some fellow activists against apartheid.

HIS EDUCATION

He obtained a Junior Certificate at the Clarkebury Boarding Institute and then started at Healdtown, a reputable Wesleyan school. He then began studying at the College of Fort Hare for his Bachelor of Arts but was unable to obtain this degree after being expelled for participating in a protest.

He then returned to Mqhekezweni and the King became furious and told him that if he did not return to school that he would find them (including Justice, who was his cousin) wives. Nelson and Justice then took off to Johannesburg, arriving in 1941. He then started working as a mining security officer where he met estate agent Walter Sisulu.

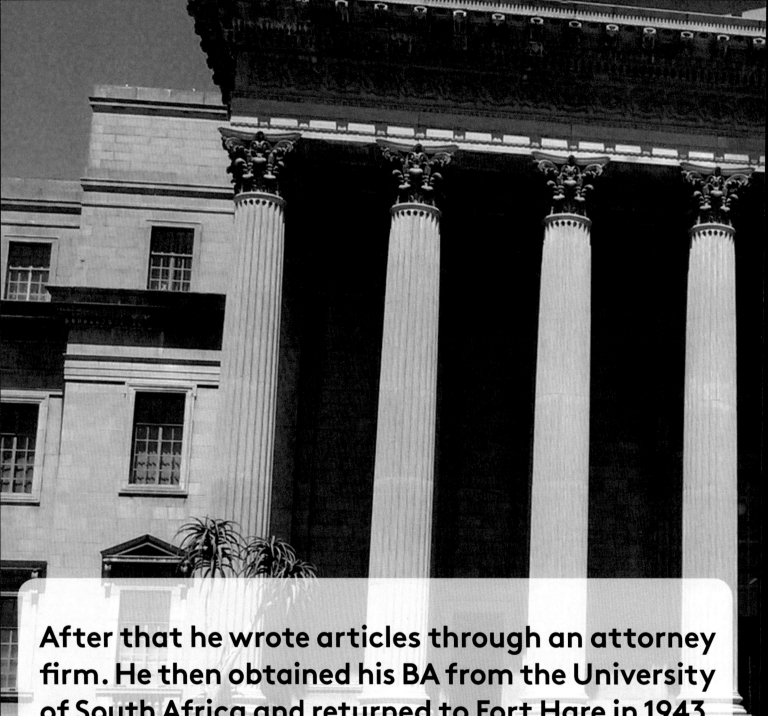

After that he wrote articles through an attorney firm. He then obtained his BA from the University of South Africa and returned to Fort Hare in 1943, to graduation.

At the same time, he started studies for his LLB at University of the Witwatersrand. He admitted to being poor student and left in 1952 without graduating.

POLITICS

While becoming increasingly involved in politics in 1942, in 1944 he became a member of the African National Congress when he assisted in creating the ANC Youth League. He married Sisulu's cousin, nurse by the name of Evelyn Mase in 1944. Two sons were then born to the family and they named them Makgatho and "Thembi" (Madiba Thembekile).

They then had two daughters, the first who died as an infant, and named them both Makaziwe. In 1958 they were divorced. He climbed up through the positions of ANCYL and due to their efforts, ANC approved a more profound mass-based strategy in 1949 called Programme of Action.

He was selected the National Volunteer-in-Chief of the Defiance Campaign in 1952, with his deputy being Maulvi Cachalia. This turned into a civil disobedience. This campaign, in opposition to six unfair laws, was between the South African Indian Congress and ANC.

They were then charged for participation in this campaign and their sentence was nine months doing hard labor, but was granted a two-year suspension. Having his BA and the diploma in law, he was allowed to practice law. Along with Oliver Tambo, they established the first black firm in South Africa, Mandela and Tambo.

THE FREEDOM CHARTER

PREAMBLE: SOUTH AFRICA BELONGS TO ALL WHO LIVE IN IT, BLACK AND WHITE AND NO GOVERNMENT CAN JUSTLY CLAIM AUTHORITY UNLESS IT IS BASED ON THE WILL OF THE PEOPLE.

1. THE PEOPLE SHALL GOVERN!
2. ALL NATIONAL GROUPS SHALL HAVE EQUAL
3. THE PEOPLE SHALL SHARE IN THE COUNTRY
4. THE LAND SHALL BE SHARED AMONG THOSE
5. ALL SHALL BE EQUAL BEFORE THE L
6. ALL SHALL ENJOY EQUAL HUMAN
7. THERE SHALL BE WORK AND SECURIT
8. THE DOORS OF LEARNING AND CULTURE SHALL BE OPENED!
9. THERE SHALL BE HOUSES, SECURIT BE LAND FRIEN
10. THERE SHALL BE

He was barred the first time at the end of 1952. As restricted, he could only secretly watch the Freedom Charter being adopted on June 25, 1955, in Kliptown.

THE TRIAL

On December 5, 1955, he was arrested in a major sweep by the police leading to the 1956 Treason Trial. Males and females of every race found themselves enduring the marathon trial that ended with the final 28 suspects, which included Mandela, finally acquitted on March 29, 1961.

April 8, 1960, police killed 69 people that were unarmed during a protest in opposition to the pass laws. This led to their first state of emergency and banned the Pan Africanist Congress, known as the PAC, and the ANC. He and his partners during this trial were among the thousands that were detained during this emergency.

On June 14, 1958, during this trial, Mandel married
Winnie Madikizela, a social worker. They went on
to conceive two daughters, Zindziswa and Zenani,
and then divorced in 1996. During the days towards
the end of the trial, he went to Pietermaritzburg in
order to talk at the All-in Africa Conference, which

that he write to Prime Minister Verwoerd asking that a national convention about a non-racial constitution and to also warn that if he did not agree they may be a strike against South Africa as a republic.

After they were acquitted, he went underground and started to plan a strike for March 29, 30 and 31. The strike ended early because of immense mobilization of the state security.

He was then asked to lead an armed struggle in June of 1961 and assisted in establishing Umkhonto weSizwe, Spear of the Nation, and this was launched on December 16, 1961 with a sequence of explosions.

Using an adopted name, David Motsamaya, on January 11, 1962, he quietly left South Africa. He traveled Africa and also went to England to obtain support for the armed struggle.

In Morocco and Ethiopa, he was able to receive military training and in 1962 he went back to South Africa.

On August 5, he was arrested in a road-block around Howick while he was returning from KwaZulu-Natal, after he discussed his trip with Albert Luthuli, the President Chief of the ANC.

They charged him with leaving the country without permission and causing the strike. He was found guilty and then began to serve his five years' sentence of imprisonment at Pretoria Local Prison.

He was transferred to Robben Island on May 27, 1963, and returned June 12 to Pretoria. Police then raided Liliesleaf within a month and several of his associates were then arrested. Liliesleaf was a hideout used by the ANC and Communist Party activists.

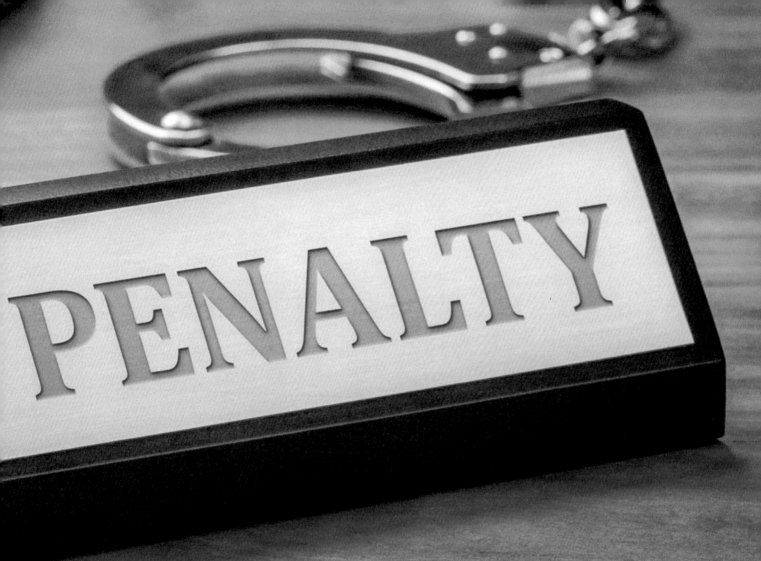

On October 9, 1963, he as well as 10 other people, were on trial for sabotage, which came to be recognized as the Rivonia Trial. As he faced the death penalty, on April 20, his words at the end of his speech became immortalized as the "Speech from the Dock."

On June 11, 1964, he and the seven others, Ahmed Kathrada, Walter Sisulu, Raymond Mhlaba, Govan Mbeki, Denis Goldberg, Andrew Mlangeni, and Elias Motsoaledi, were found guilty and on the next day they found out their sentence to be life imprisonment.

Since he was white, Golberg was sent to Pretoria Prison, and the others were sent to Robben Island. His mother passed away in 1968 and his older son, Thembi, passed away in 1969. He was not permitted to go to their funerals. He was send to Pollsmoor Prison on March 31, 1982, along with Mlangeni, Sisulu, and Mhlaba then in October Kathrada joined them.

After recovering from prostate surgery in November of 1985, he was retained alone. Justice Minister Kobie Coetsee saw him at the hospital. He later started discussion while ultimately led to a meeting between the ANC and apartheid government.

RELEASE FROM PRISON

He was diagnosed with tuberculosis on August 12, 1988, after a visit to the hospital. After two hospitals in three months, he was then transferred to Victor Verster Prison on December 7, 1988, where he stayed during the last of the 14 months of his imprisonment.

ORDER FOR RELEASE
OF PRISONER ON BA

THE PEOPLE OF THE STATE OF

VS

FEDERAL RES

HA 24302
A1

He was then released on February 11, 1990, only nine days after the PAC and the ANC were unbanned, and approximately four months after release of his remaining colleagues. Throughout his imprisonment, he rebuffed at least three provisional offers for release. He then immersed

into talks to end the white minority rule and was then elected ANC President in 1991, replacing Oliver Tambo, his friend who had been taken ill. In 1993, he then won the Nobel Peace Prize, jointly with President FW de Klerk and proceeded to vote for the first time on April 27, 1994.

HIS PRESIDENCY

He was inaugurated on May 10, 1994 as the first President of South Africa to be elected democratically. In 1998, On his 80th birthday, he was married to wife number three, Graca Machel.

Nelson Mandela

In 1999, he stepped down after only one term. He continued his effort with the Nelson Mandela Children's Fund and started The Mandela Rhodes Foundation and the Nelson Mandela Foundation.

Mandla, Mandela, his grandson, was instated as the head of Mvezo Traditional Council at Mvezo Great Place in April of 2007. His devotion to equality, learning and democracy never wavered.

STOP RACISM

Even with horrible provocation, he would never answer racism with racism. His life is an encouragement to anyone that deprived and oppressed; and to anyone in opposition to deprivation and oppression. On December 5, 2013, he died in Johannesburg, at home.

To learn more about Nelson Mandela, research the internet, go to your local library, and asked questions to your teachers, family, and friends.

DISSECTED LIVES
auto biographies

www.DissectedLives.Com